Italian

Phrase Book

(Second Edition)

JANE WIGHTWICK

New York Chicago San Francisco Lisbon London Madrid Mexico City
Milan New Delhi San Juan Seoul Singapore Sydney Toronto

About this book

Jane Wightwick
had the idea

Wina Gunn
wrote the pages

Leila & Zeinah Gaafar
(aged 10 and 12) drew the
first pictures in each
chapter

Robert Bowers
(aged 56) drew the other
pictures, and
designed the book

Marc Vitale
did the Italian stuff

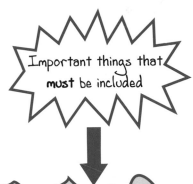

Important things that **must** be included

1 2 3 4 5 6 7 8 9 0   09 10 11 12

ISBN 978-0-07-161585-3
MHID 0-07-161585-7

McGraw-Hill books are available at special quantity discounts to use as premiums and sales promotions or for use in corporate training programs. To contact a representative, please visit the Contact Us pages at www.mhprofessional.com.

This book is printed on acid-free paper.

Printed and bound by Tien Wah Press, Singapore.

What's inside

Making friends

How to be cool with the group

Wanna play?

Our guide to joining in everything from hide-and-seek to the latest electronic game

Feeling hungry

Order your favorite foods or go local

Looking good

Make sure you keep up with all those essential fashions

anging out

At the pool, beach, or theme park—don't miss out on the action

ocket money

Spend it here!

rown-up talk

blah!
blah!
blah!
blah!

If you really, really have to!

xtra stuff

All the handy things—numbers, months, time, days of the week

my big brother il mio fratello grande
eel meeyo fratel-loh granday

grandpa nonno
non-noh

grandma nonna
non-nah

papà
pa-pah

mom mamma
mam-mah

my little sister
la mia sorellina
la meeya sorel-leenah

Half a step this way

stepfather/stepmother
patrigno/matrigna
👄 patreenio/matreenia

step-son/step-daughter
figliastro/figliastra
👄 feelyeeastroh/feelyeeastrah

step-brother/step-sister
fratellastro/sorellastra
👄 fratel-lastroh/sorel-lastrah

Hi! Ciao!
👄 chee-ow

What's your name?
Come ti chiami?
👄 komay tee kee-amee

My name's ...
Mi chiamo ...
👄 mee kee-amoh

The word **ciao** means "hello" <u>and</u> "goodbye" – it's such a famous word you might already use it with your American friends. You can say **Ciao, come va?** (*chee-ow, komay vah*, "Hi, how's it going?") or **Ciao, ci vediamo!** (*chee-ow, chee vaydee-amoh*, "Bye, see you later!")

from Canada
dal Canada
👄 dal kana-da

from Ireland
dall'Irlanda
👄 dal-leerland

from Scotland
dalla Scozia
👄 dal-la skotseea

from Wales
dal Galles
👄 dal gal-les

from the U.S.
dagli Stati Uniti
👄 dalyee statee uneetee

from England
dall'Inghilterra
👄 dal-lingilter-ra

SMS

dv 6? mi rsp all'sms xche dm devo vedere qlk1. tvb cmq

Bet you're thinking — Italian texts don't make any sense! But remember an Italian "1" is pronounced "oono" and a 6 is pronounced "say." The Italian word for "times" as in 2x2 is "per", so "perché" (because/why) becomes "xche." Get it now? ... hehehe!

dv 6? *(dove sei)*
wru?

xche *(perché)*
cos/y

mi rsp *(mi rispondi)*
txt me

qlk1 *(qualcuno)*
sum1

sms
xt

tvb *(ti voglio tanto bene)*
luv

dm *(domani)*
2moro

cmq *(comunque)*
anyway

hehehe
lol

How old are you?

Quanti anni hai?

👄 kwantee an-nee eye

12 years old

Dodici anni

👄 dodeechee an-nee

Happy birthday! Buon compleanno!

👄 boo-on komplayan-no

What's your star sign?

Di che segno sei?

👄 dee kay sayneeo say

When's your birthday?

Quando è il tuo compleanno

👄 kwando ay eel too-oh komplayan-no

Star Signs

AQUARIUS

Jan. 21 – Feb. 19
...ario 👄 ak-kwareeoh

PISCES

Feb. 20 – Mar. 20
Pesci 👄 payshi

ARIES

Mar. 21 – Apr. 20
Ariete 👄 aree-aytay

TAURUS
Apr. 21 – May 21
Toro 👄 toroh

GEMINI

May 22 – June 21
Gemelli 👄 jaymel-lee

CANCER
June 22 – July 23
Cancro 👄 kank-roh

LEO
July 24 – Aug. 23
Leone 👄 layonay

VIRGO

Aug. 24 – Sep. 23
Vergine 👄 vaurjeenay

LIBRA
Sep. 24 – Oct. 23
Bilancia 👄 beelancheea

SCORPIO

Oct. 24 – Nov. 22
...rpione 👄 skorpeeonay

SAGITTARIUS

Nov. 23 – Dec. 21
Sagittario 👄 sajeet-tareeo

CAPRICORN

Dec. 22 – Jan. 20
Capricorno 👄 kapreecorno

13

14

soccer il calcio
👄 kalchee-oh

rollerblading
il pattinaggio
👄 pat-teenaj-jeeoh

music
la musica
👄 moozikah

electronic games
i giochi elettronici
👄 ee jee-okee
aylet-tr-roneechee

la tela
👄 la taylay

comics
i fumetti
👄 ee foomayt-tee

school la scuola
👄 la skwolah

spiders i ragni
👄 ee ranyee

15

What's ...?
Qual è ...?
👄 kwalay

your favorite group
il tuo complesso preferito
👄 eel too-oh komples-
soh pray-fayreetoh

your favorite color
il tuo colore preferito
👄 eel too-oh koloray
pray-fayreetoh

→ Page 69

your favorite game
il tuo gioco preferito
👄 eel too-oh jee-oko
pray-fayreetoh

your favorite food
il tuo cibo preferito
👄 eel too-oh cheeboh
pray-fayreetoh

ur favorite ring tone
tua suoneria preferita
👄 la too-ah soo-onereeyah
pray-fayreetah

your favorite animal
il tuo animale preferito
👄 eel too-oh aneemalay
pray-fayreetoh

your favorite team
la tua squadra preferita
👄 la too-ah skwadra
pray-fayreetah

Talk about your pets

He's hungry
È affamato
👄 ay afah-maytoh

She's sleeping
Sta dormendo
👄 stah dormendoh

Can I pet your dog?
Posso accarezzare il tuo cane?
👄 possoh akaraytzarau too-oh kanay

Do you have any pets?
Hai qualche animali?
👄 eye kwalkay aneemah-lee

cat
il gatto
 eel gat-toh

dog il cane
 eel kanay

snake
il serpente
 eel sairpayntay

guinea-pig
il porcellino d'India
 eel porchel-leenoh
deendeea

hamster
il criceto
 eel crichaytoh

budgie
il pappagallino
eel pap-pagal-leenoh

My little doggy goes *"bau bau"*!

An Italian doggy doesn't say "woof, woof," it says **bau, bau** (*baoo, baoo*). An Italian bird says **pio, pio** (*pee-o, pee-o*) and a "cock-a-doodle-do" in Italian chicken-speak is **chichirichì** (*keek-kee ree-kee*). But a cat does say "miao" and a cow "moo" whether they're speaking Italian or English!

19

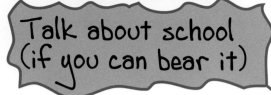

Talk about school (if you can bear it)

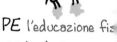

geography
la geografia
👄 lah jayografeea

PE l'educazione fis...
👄 laydooka-tseec...
feezeekah

art l'educazione artistica
👄 laydooka-tseeonay
arteesteekah

Italian
m.smith
form 2b

Italian
l'italiano
👄 leetaleeano

$\sqrt{E} + (.42 = ...$
$= x \div c^2$

math
la matematica
👄 la matay-mateeka...

English
l'inglese
👄 leenglayzay

English
m.smith
I love sandra x
x

music
la musica
👄 la moozeekah

science scienze
👄 lay shee-enzy

history
la storia
👄 la storeeah

IT

il computer
👄 eel "computer"

Way unfair!

Italian children hardly ever have to wear uniform to school nowadays (but in primary school they used to wear overalls, white with a big blue bow for girls and blue with a big white bow for boys!). Summer vacations are very long, sometimes even up to 12 weeks. But before you turn green with envy, you might not like the dreaded **ripetizioni** (*reepay-teetsee-onee*) or "vacation classes," which you have to take if you fail your end-of-year exams.

And if your marks are really bad the teachers could make you repeat the whole year with your little sister!

Talk about your phone

That's ancient!
Che vecchio!
👄 kay vekyoh

I've run out of credit
Ho finito i soldi
👄 oh fineetoh ee soldee

What's your phone like?
Com'è il tuo telefonino?
👄 komay eel too-oh taylayfoneenoh

Lucky!
Sei troppo fortunato!
👄 say troppo fortoon-atoh

What a great ring tone!
Che bella la tua suoneria!
👄 kay bella lah too-ah soo-onereeyah

23

Gossip

Can you keep a secret?

Sai mantenere un segreto?

👄 sah-ee mantaynayray oon saygretoh

Do you have a boyfriend (a girlfriend)?

Ce l'hai il ragazzo (la ragazza)?

👄 chay l'eye eel ragatsoh (lah ragatsah)

An OK guy/An OK girl

Un tipo simpatico/Una tipa simpatica

👄 oon teepo seempateekoh/ oona teepa seempateekah

Way bossy!

Che prepotente!

👄 kay praypotayntay

He's nutty/She's nutty!

È uno svitato/È una svitata!

👄 ay oono sveetatoh/ ay oona sveetatah

svitato means "unscrewed"!

What a complainer!

Che lagna!

👄 kay laneea

24

You won't make many friends saying this!

Bug off!
Levati dai piedi!
👄 layvatee die peeaydee

That means "get off my feet"!

Shut up! **Sta' zitto!**
👄 stah dzeet-toh

You're fed up with someone, and you want to say something like "you silly …!" or "you stupid …!" you can start with **testa di** (which actually means "head of …") and add anything you like. The most common are:

or …

Cabbage head!
Testa di cavolo!
taystah dee kavoloh

Turnip head!
Testa di rapa!
taystah dee rapah

Take your pick. You could also start with **pezzo di** … ("piece of …") and say **pezzo d'idiota!** (*paytso deedeeotah*). You don't need a translation here, do you?

You might have to say

Rat.
Mannaggi
👄 man-naj-jee...

Fudge!
Uffa!
👄 oof-fah

That's not funny
Non fa ridere nessuno
👄 non fah reedayray
nesoonoh

I'm fed up
Sono stufo! (boys)
Sono stufa! (girls)
👄 sono stoofoh
👄 sono stoofah

That's enough!
Basta così!
👄 bastah kozee

26

Stop it! *Smettila!*
👄 smayt-teela

I want to go home!
Voglio tornare a casa
👄 volyoh tornaray ah kaza

I don't care
Non me ne importa niente
👄 non may nay importah neeayntay

At last!
Finalmente!
👄 feenalmayntay

Saying goodbye

What's your address?
Qual è il tuo indirizzo?
👄 kwalay eel too-oh een-deereetso

Here's my address
Ecco il mio indirizzo
👄 ekko eel meeo een-deereetso

Come to visit me
Vieni a trovarmi
👄 vee-aynee ah trovarmee

Have a good trip!
Buon viaggio!
👄 bwon veeajeeoh

Write to me soon
Scrivimi presto
👄 skreeveemee praystoh

Send me a text
Mandami un messaggio
👄 mandamee oon messah-jeeyo

Do you like chatting online?
Hai voglia di chattare?
👄 eye volyah dee chattaray

Bye!
Ciao!
👄 chee-ow

What's your email address?
Qual è la tua mail?
👄 kwalay la too-ah mail

⊃□@3◇*@ℛ.com

29

WANNA PLAY?

l'elastico 👄 laylasteeko

il ping-pong
👄 eel peeng-pong

il lettore
🗪 eel laytoray

lo yo-yo
🗪 loh "yo-yo"

il telefonino
🗪 eel taylay-
foneenoh

WANNA PLAY?

Do you want to play ...?
Vuoi giocare ...?
👄 voo-oi jokaray

... foos-ball?
... a calcetto?
👄 ah kal-chayt-toh

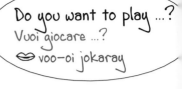

... cards?
... a carte?
👄 ah kartay

... on the computer?
... al computer?
👄 al komputer

... hangman?
... all'impiccato?
👄 al-leempeek-katoh

... hide-and-seek?
... a nascondino?
👄 ah naskondeenoh

... catch?
... a palla?
👄 ah pal-lah

Not now
Adesso no
👄 adays-so noh

Yeah, let's!
Sì, giochiamo!
👄 see, jeeokee-amoh

33

Care for a game of **leap the foal** or **pretty statues**?

In Italy, tag is called **chiapparello** (*kiap-parel-loh*), which sort of means "catchy-poos"! And instead of leap frog, Italian children play leap "foal" – **la cavallina** (*lah caval-leenah*). Another very popular game is **belle statuine** (*bellay statoo-eenay*) or "pretty statues," which is similar to "big bad wolf." When someone is standing around doing nothing Italians will often ask "Are you playing pretty statues?" – **Fai la bella statuina?** (*fie lah bellah statoo-eenah*).

Can my friend play too?
Può giocare anche il mio amico?
👄 poo-o jeeokaray ankay eel mee-yo ameekoh

I have to ask my parents
Devo chiedere ai
👄 dayvoh keeea~ dayray eye mee~

34

Who dares?

You're it!
Stai sotto tu!
👄 sty sot-to too

Race you?
Facciamo una corsa?
👄 facheeamoh oona
korsah

I'm first
Sono primo io (boy)
Sono prima io (girl)
👄 sonoh preemoh eeo
sonoh preemah eeo

Electronic games

lo schermo
👄 loh skayrmoh

il modem
👄 eel "modem"

il CD-Rom
👄 eel chee-dee ror

HIGH SCORES

Frank
Robert
Leila
Sarah
Jean-Paul
Denis
Wina
Jane

il mouse
👄 eel "mo

la tastiera
👄 la tasteeayrah

il microfono
👄 eel meek-rofonoh

le cuffie
👄 lay kufyay

38

Show me
Fammi vedere
👄 fam-mee vaydayray

What do I do?
Che devo fare?
👄 kay dayvoh faray

Am I dead?
Sono morto?
👄 sonoh mortoh

Shoot-em-up!
Spara!
👄 sparah

How many lives do I have?
Quante vite ho?
👄 kwantay veetay oh

How many levels are there?
Quanti livelli ci sono?
👄 kwantee leevayl-lee chee sonoh

It's virtual fun!

Do you have a webcam?
ce l'hai una webcam
👄 chay l'eye oona "webcam"

Send me a message.
Mandami un messaggio.

How do I join?
Come m'iscrivo?

I'm not old enough.
Non sono grande abbastanza.

I'm not allowed.
Non mi è permesso.

I don't know who you are.
Non so chi sei.

my blog
il mio blog
👄 eel meeyo
"blog"

my friends
i miei amici
👄 ee mee–ay ameechee

my photos
la mie foto
👄 lay mee–ay fotoh

videos
iei video
👄 ee mee–ay vee–dayoh

music la mia musica
👄 la meeyah moosikah

41

hockey
l'hockey
👄 lok-kay

gymnastics
la ginnastica
👄 la jeen-nasteekah

ballet
la danza classica
👄 la dantsa
klas-seekah

basketball
la pallacanestro
👄 la pal-lakanaystrah

...d, of course, we haven't forgotten "*il calcio*" ... (P.T.O.) **43**

soccer

cleats
gli scarponcini
👄 lyee skarponcheenee

soccer gear
la divisa da calcio
👄 lah deeveezah dah kalch

ref
l'arbitro
👄 larbeetroh

shin pads
i parastinchi
👄 ee parasteenkee

Good save!
Ben parato!
👄 ben paratoh

44

Pass! Passa!
👄 pas-sah

Offside!
Fuori gioco!
👄 foo-oree jeeoko

Hands!
Fallo di mano!
👄 fal-lo dee mano

You're on my team
Tu sei con noi
👄 too say kon noy

crossbar
traversa
👄 la travayrsah

goalpost
il palo
👄 eel palo

goal
la porta
👄 la portah

goalie
il portiere
👄 eel porteeayray

45

Keeping the others in line

Not like that!
Cosi no!
👄 kozee noh

You cheat! Sei un imbroglione! (boys only)
Sei un'imbrogliona! (girls only)
👄 say oon eembrolyee-onay
say oon eembrolyee-onah

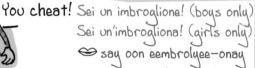

I'm not playing anymore
Non gioco più
👄 non jeeoko peeoo

Stop it!
Smettila!
👄 smayt-teela

It's not fair!
Non vale!
👄 non valay

47

Showing off

... do a handstand?
... fare la verticale?
👄 faray la vayrteecalay

Can you ...
Sai ...
👄 sah-ee

Look at me!
Guardatemi!
👄 gooardataymee

... do a cartwheel?
... fare la ruota?
👄 faray la roo-otah

... do this?
... fare questo?
👄 faray kways

48

Tongue tied

Impress your Italian friends with this!

Show off to your new Italian friends by practising this **cioglilingua** (*shee-olyeleen-gooa*), or tongue twister:

Sopra la panca la capra campa, sotto la panca la capra crepa.

soprah la pankah la kaprah kampah, sot-toh la pankah la kaprah kraypah

(This means "On the bench the goat lives, under the bench the goat dies.")

Then see if they can do as well with this English one:

"She sells seashells on the seashore, but the shells she sells aren't seashells, I'm sure."

For a rainy day

deck of cards
mazzo di carte
👄 matso dee kartay

my deal/your deal
do io le carte/
dai tu le carte
👄 dahray eo lay kartay
die too lay kartay

king il re
👄 eel ray

queen
la regina
👄 la rayjeen

jack il fante
👄 eel fantay

joker il jolly
👄 eel jol-lee

fiori
👄 feeoree

cuori
👄 koo-oree

picche
👄 peek-kay

quadri
👄 kwadre

50

Do you have the ace of swords?!

You may see Italian children playing with a different pack of cards. There are only 40 cards instead of 52 and the suits are also different. Instead of clubs, spades, diamonds and hearts, there are gold coins (**denari** *daynaree*), swords (**spade** *spahday*), cups (**coppe** *oppay*) and sticks (**bastoni** *bastonee*).

chessboard la scacchiera
👄 la skak-keeayrah

l'alfiere
👄 lalfeeayray

il cavallo
👄 eel kaval-loh

pedone
👄 eel paydonay

la torre
👄 lah torray

la regina
👄 lah rayjeeanah

il re 👄 eel ray

squid
i calamari
👄 ee kalamaree

mussels
le cozze
👄 lay kotsay

caramel custard
crème caramel
👄 eel krem karamel

orange juice
il succo d'arancia
👄 eel sook-koh
darancheeah

FEELING HUNGRY

Grub

I'm starving
Ho una fame da lupo
👄 oh oona famay dah
loopoh

That means "I have the hunger of a wolf!"

il lupo

Please can I have ...
Mi dà ...
👄 mee dah

54

... a croissant

... un cornetto

👄 oon cornayt-toh

... a chocolate pastry

... un pasticcino al cioccolato

👄 oon pasteech-cheeno al chok-kolatoh

... a sandwich

... un tramezzino

👄 oon tramay-dzeeno

... a slice of pizza

... un pezzo di pizza

👄 oon paytso dee peetsa

... a calzone

... un calzone

👄 oon caltsonay

55

In the winter, you can buy bags of delicious roasted chestnuts from street sellers, hot and ready to eat!

a bag of chestnuts
un cartoccio di castagne
👄 oon kartocheeo dee kastaneeay

Take-away pizza in Italy is often sold **al taglio** (*al talyee-oh*), which means it is cut into rectangular slices from a large baking sheet … and you can buy as big a piece as you like. Another great midday snack is a **calzone** (*caltsonay*), which is a round pizza folded in half with all the juicy bits inside.

If you want something really cold and slushy in the summer you can ask for **una granita** *(oona graneetah)*, which is crushed ice with fruit juice or syrup.

water
acqua
👄 akkwah

a milkshake
un frullato
👄 oon frool-latoh

a syrup
uno sciroppo
👄 oonoh sheerop-poh

If you're really lucky you might go to Italy during **Carnevale** in February. Adults and kids dress up in the weirdest costumes and everyone goes loopy for a few days. There are lots of special sticky cakes like *frappe* *(frappay)*: big pastry bows dipped in icing sugar; and **castagnole** *(kastanyolay)*: delicious fried balls of pastry covered in sugar.

You: Can I have some castagnole, Mum?

Mom: No. They'll make you fat and rot your teeth.

You: But I think it's good to experience a foreign culture through authentic local food.

Mom: Oh, all right then.

Pasta Pasta Pasta!

Italians, especially those from Naples, claim to have invented pasta (we know it really grows on trees!). There are lots of different types of pasta and just as many, if not more, different sauces to go with them, including a sauce made with squid ink! You have probably heard of **spaghetti** and **tagliatelle**, but what about these:

penne (quills)

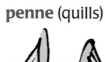

farfalle (butterflies)

ruote (wheels)

lumache (snails!)

 stelline (little stars)

Parties

balloon
il palloncino
👄 eel paloncheeno

Can I have some more?
Potrei averne un altro po'?
👄 potray avairnay oon altroh po

party hat
il cappello da festa
👄 eel kap-pello dah festa

This is for you
Questo è per te
👄 kwaysto ay payr tay

What do Italian children play at birthday parties?

Pasta parcel!

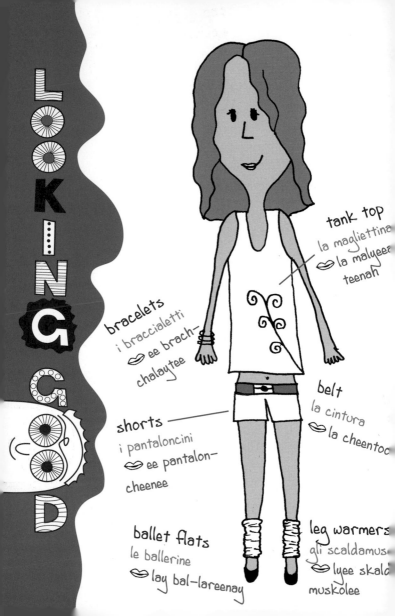

sweatshirt
la felpa
🗣 la faylpah

cap
il berretto
🗣 eel ber–rayt–toh

tattoo
il tatuaggio
🗣 eel tatooaj–jeeo

jeans
i jeans
🗣 ee jeens

tennis shoes
gli scarponcini
🗣 lyee skarponcheenee

LOOKING GOOD

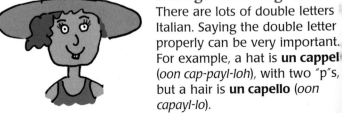

She's got an orange hair!
There are lots of double letters Italian. Saying the double letter properly can be very important. For example, a hat is **un cappel** (*oon cap-payl-loh*), with two "p"s, but a hair is **un capello** (*oon capayl-lo*).

spotted
a pois
👄 ah pooah

flowery
a fiori
👄 ah feeoree

frilly
con i fronzoli
👄 kon ee frondzolee

glittery
luccicante
👄 luch-cheekantay

striped
a strisce
👄 ah streeshay

65

Clothes

jeans
i jeans
👄 ee jeens

sweatshi
la felpa
👄 la fay

T-shirt
la maglietta
👄 lah malyeeayt—

soccer jersey
la maglietta da calcio
👄 lah malyeeayt-tah
da calcheeo

tennis shoes
gli scarponcini
👄 lyee skar-
poncheenee

66

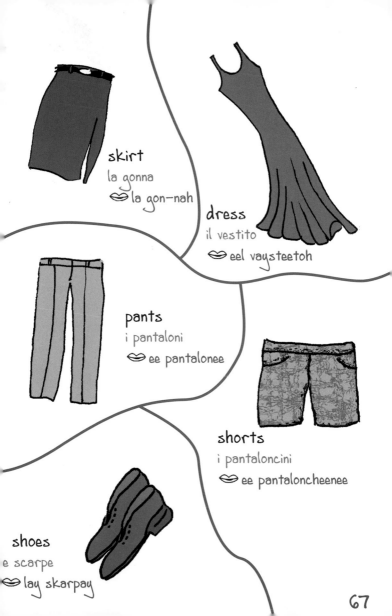

skirt
la gonna
👄 la gon-nah

dress
il vestito
👄 eel vaysteetoh

pants
i pantaloni
👄 ee pantalonee

shorts
i pantaloncini
👄 ee pantaloncheenee

shoes
e scarpe
👄 lay skarpay

67

Make it up!

lip gloss
il lucidalabbra
👄 eel loocheeda labrah

glitter gel
il gel luccicante
👄 eel "gel" luch– cheekantay

nail polish
lo smalto per le unghie
👄 lo smalto payr lay ungyay

earrings gli orecchini
👄 lyee oraykeenee

I need a mirror
Mi serve uno specchio
👄 mee servay oono spek–kyo

eye shadow
l'ombretto
👄 lombrayt–to

Can you lend me your flat iron?
Me lo presti il tuo lisciacapelli?
👄 may lo prestee eel too–oh leesheeya–kapayllee

68

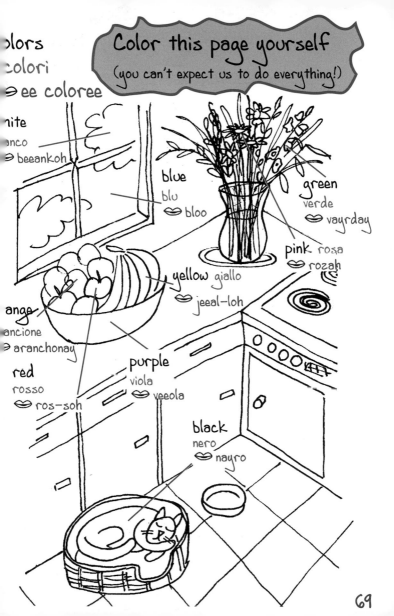

colors
colori
👄 ee coloree

Color this page yourself
(you can't expect us to do everything!)

white
bianco
👄 beeankoh

blue
blu
👄 bloo

green
verde
👄 vayrday

pink rosa
👄 rozah

yellow giallo
👄 jeeal-loh

orange
arancione
👄 aranchonay

purple
viola
👄 veeola

red
rosso
👄 ros-soh

black
nero
👄 nayro

69

What should we do?

Che facciamo?

👄 kay facheeamoh

Can I come too?

Vengo anch'io?

👄 vayngo ankeeoh

Where do you all hang out?

Dove v'incontrate?

👄 dovay veenkontratay

That's really wicked

Che forte

👄 kay fortay

I'm not allowed

Non mi lasciano

👄 non mee lasheeanoh

Let's go back

Torniamo indietro

👄 torneeamoh indeeaytroh

It gives me goose bumps (or "goose flesh" in Italian!)

Mi fa venire la pelle d'oca

👄 mee fah vayneeray la payl-lay dokah

I'm bored to death

Sto morendo dalla noia

👄 stoh morayndoh dal-la noya

That's funny

Quello è buffissimo

👄 kwel-lo ay boof-fees-seemoh

73

Beach bums

Can I borrow this?
Me lo presti?
👄 may loh praystee

Let's hit the bea[ch]
Tutti al mare
👄 toot-tee al ma[re]

Is this your bucket?
È tuo questo secchiello?
👄 ay too-o kwestoh saykeeayl-lo

You can bury me
Mi puoi seppellire
👄 mee poo-oee sayp-payl-leeray

Stop throwing sand!
Smetti di tirare la sabbia!
👄 smayt-tee dee teeraray la sab-beeah

Watch out for my ey[es]
Non mi buttare la sabbia negli occhi!
👄 non mee boot-taray l[a] sab-beea nelyee ok-kee

74

sandcastle
castello di sabbia
👄 eel kastayl-loh dee sa-beeah

sea
il mare
👄 eel maray

beach
la spiaggia
👄 la speeaj-jah

towel
l'asciugamano
👄 lashoogamanoh

bathing suit
il costume da bagno
👄 eel kostoomay dah banyeeoh

bucket
il secchiello
👄 eel sayk-keeayl-loh

snorkel
boccaglio
👄 eel bok-kaleeyo

shells
le conchiglie
👄 lay konkeelyeeay

shovel
la paletta
👄 la palayt-tah

75

It's going swimmingly!

How to make a splash in Italian!

PLUF

Let's hit the swimming pool
Tutti in piscina
👄 toot-tee een peesheena

Can you swim (underwater)?
Sai nuotare (sott'acqua
👄 saee nwotar (sot-takwa

Me too/ I can't
Anch'io/Io no
👄 ankeeo/eeo noh

Can you dive?
Ti sai tuffare?
👄 tee sah-ee toof-faray

I'm getting changed
Mi sto cambiando
👄 mee stoh kambeeandoh

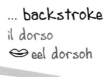

... backstroke
il dorso
👄 eel dorsoh

Can you do ...?
Sai fare ...?
👄 sah-ee faray

... butterfly
la farfalla
👄 la farfal-la

... crawl
il stile libero
👄 eel steelay leebayroh

... breaststroke
la rana 👄 la ranah

[which means "the frog," and, let's face it, that's what you look like!]

slide
lo scivolo
👄 loh sheevoloh

goggles gli occhialini
👄 lyee ok-keealeenee

Italy has a high-speed train called the **Pendolino**, which means 'leaning over' because the carriage lean to the side when it speeds roun bends. Persuade you parents to try it – it's better than a roller-coaster!

Do you know the way?
Sai la strada?
👄 sah-ee la stradah

Let's ask
Chiediamo
👄 kyee-aydeeamoh

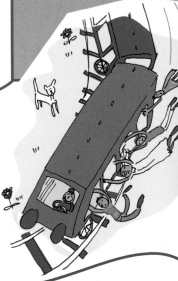

bus l'autobus
👄 laootoboos

Is it far?
È lontano? 👄 ay lontanoh

Are we allowed in here?
Possiamo entrare?
👄 pos-seeamoh ayntraray

car la macchina
👄 lah mak-keenah

The "proper" Italian word for car is **automobile** (*aootomobee-ay*) but you'll look much cooler if you say **macchina** (*mak-keenah*) or, if the car has seen better days, **macinino** (*macheeneenoh*). Use the cooler short words instead of those long untrendy ones the adults will try and make you say: **bici** (*beechee*) instead of **bicicletta**, **moto** instead of **motocicletta** and **bus** (*boos*) instead of **autobus**.

Park yourself here

swings
le altalene
👄 lay altalayna

jungle gym
il quadro svedese
👄 eel kwadro zveday:

playground
il parco giochi
👄 eel parko jeeokee

grass il prato
👄 eel prato

tree l'albero
👄 lalbayro

slide
lo scivolo
👄 lo sheevolo

80

park il parco 👄 eel park

Can we play ball games?
Giochiamo a palla
👄 jeeokee-ahmo a palla

merry-go-round
la giostra
👄 la gee-ostra

sandbox la sabbia
👄 la sab-beeya

Can I have a go?
Mi fai provare
👄 mee faee provaray

81

Picnics

I hate wasps
Odio le vespe
👄 odeeo lay
vayspay

Move over!
Fatti più in là!
👄 fat-tee
peeoo een lah

bread
il pane 👄 eel panay

Let's sit her
Sediamoci a
👄 saydeeamochee kw

napkin
il tovagliolo
👄 eel tovalyeeolo

ham il prosciutto
👄 eel proshoot-to

cheese
il formaggio
👄 eel formaj-je

yogurt
lo yogurt
👄 loh yogoort

chips
le patatine
👄 lay patateenau

82

drinks
le bibite
👄 lay beebeetay

knife
il coltello
👄 eel koltayl-lo

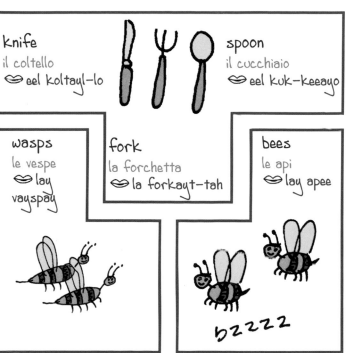

spoon
il cucchiaio
👄 eel kuk-keeayo

wasps
le vespe
👄 lay vayspay

fork
la forchetta
👄 la forkayt-tah

bees
le api
👄 lay apee

bzzzz

ants
le formiche
👄 lay formeekay

Wake up, campers!

tent la tenda
👄 la taynda

tent peg
il picchetto
👄 eel peek-kayt-

camper van
il camper
👄 eel "camper"

penknife
il coltellino svizzero
👄 eel koltayl-leeno
zveet-tzayro

stove
il fornello
👄 eel fornayllo

sleeping bag il sacco a pelo
👄 eel sakko a paylo

flashlight la torc
👄 la torcheeya

84

That tent's a palace! Quella tenda è un palazzo!
🗣 kwella taynda ay oon palat-zoh

Campfire
fuoco d'accampamento
🗣 eel foo-oko
akampa-maynto

I've lost my flashlight
Ho perso la mia torcia
🗣 oh payrso la meeya
torcheeya

The showers are gross
Le docce fanno schifo!
🗣 lay dotchay fanno
skeefo

Where does the garbage go?
Dove va la spazzatura?
🗣 dovay vah la spatza-toorah

All the fun of the fair

Ferris wheel la ruota panoramica
👄 la rwotah panorameeka

slide lo scivolo
👄 loh sheevolo

house of mirrors
la casa degli specchi
👄 la kasah delyee spayk-kee

bumper cars l'autoscontro
👄 laootoskontro

Let's try this
Andiamo su questo
👄 andeeamo soo

kwesto

Disco nights

mirror ball
la palla specchiata
👄 la palla spayk-kyata

loudspeaker
la cassa
👄 la kas-sa

Can I request a song?
Posso chiedere una canzone?
👄 posso kee-ayderay oona kanzonay

The music is really lame
La musica è troppo noiosa
👄 la mooseeka ay troppo noyosa

spotlight
lo spot
👄 loh "spot"

DJ il DJ
👄 eel "DJ"

turntable
la piattaforma giran
👄 la pyattaforma geerantay

88

How old do I need to be?

Quanti anni devo avere?
👄 kwantee annee dayvo averay

dance floor

la pista da ballo
👄 la peesta dah ballo

Shall we dance?

Balliamo?
👄 bal-lyahmo

I love this song!

Questa canzone mi fa impazzire!
👄 kwaysta kanzonay mee fah impat-zeeray

89

POCKET MONEY

candy
le caramelle
lay karamayl-lay

T-shirts
le magliette
lay male
eeayt-tay

toys
i giocattoli
ee jeeokat-tolee

shop assistant
il commesso
eel kom-mays-

books
i libri
👄 ee leebree

il mobile
👄 eel "mobile"

pencils
le matite
👄 lay mateetay

POCKET MONEY

What does that sign say?

Macelleria

macelleria
butcher shop
👄 machayl-layreeah

pasticceria
cake shop
👄 pastee-chayreeah

Pasticceria

panetteria
bakery
👄 panayt-tayreea

Panetteria

negozio di dolciumi
candy store
👄 naygotseeo dee dolcheeoomee

Fruttivendolo

Cartoleria

cartoleria
office supplies
👄 kartolayreeah

fruttivendolo
fruit and veget store 👄 froot-teevayndoloh

negozio di abbigliamento
clothes shop
👄 naygotseeo dee ab-beelyeeamaynto

Do you have some dosh?
Ce l'hai qualche soldo?
👄 chay lie kwalkay soldo

I'm broke
Sono al verde
👄 sono al vayrday

I'm loaded
Sono ricco sfondato
👄 sono reek-ko sfondato

Here you go
Tieni
👄 teeaynee

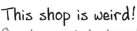

This shop is weird!
Questo negozio è strano!
👄 kwesto naygotseeo ay stah-no

That's a bargain È un affare
👄 ay oon af-faray

It's a rip off!
Questi ti spellano!
👄 kwaystee tee spayl-lanoh

93

Sweet heaven!

I love this shop
Adoro questo negozio
👄 adohro kwesto naygotseeo

Let's get some candy
Prendiamo delle caramelle
👄 prayndeeamo dayllay karamayl-lay

Let's get an ice cream
Prendiamo un gelato
👄 prayndeeamo oon jaylatoh

lollipops *lecca lecca*
👄 lek-kah lek-kah
[that means "lick-lick"!]

a bar of chocolat[e]
una tavoletta di cioccolat[a]
👄 oona tavolayt-tah d[e] chok-kolatah

chewing gum
gomma da masticare
👄 gom-mah dah masteekaray

If you really want to look Italian (but end up with lots of fillings) try these:

baci Perugina
(bachee peroo-jeenah)

The most famous Italian chocolate has to be **baci Perugina** (literally "kisses"), nuggets of chocolate and nuts wrapped in silver paper with little romantic messages for that boy or girl you like!

rbone di zucchero
rbonay dee dzook-kayro)!

gar coal. On 6th January, the Epiphany, lian kids get presents, but those who ve been naughty get coal! Actually this black coal-shaped candy – phew!

pecorelle di zucchero
(paykorayl-lay dee dzook-kayro).

Forget the Easter eggs, try some 'little sugar sheep'!

nder sorpresa
nder sorpraysah)

u probably know these inder Surprise" chocolate eggs th wicked little toys, but did u know they come from Italy?

95

Other things you could buy

(that won't rot your teeth!)

What are you getting?
Tu che prendi?
👄 too kay prayndee

That toy, plea[s...]
Quel giocattolo, per favor[e]
👄 kwayl jeeokat-tol[o]
payr favor[e]

Two postcards, please
Due cartoline, per favore
👄 dooay
kartoleenay
payr favoray

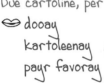

This is garbage
Questa è robaccia
👄 kwesta ay
robach-cha

This is cool
Questo è eccezionale
👄 kwesto ay echetseeonalay

I'm getting ...
Io prendo ...
👄 eeo prendoh

... a pen
... una penna
👄 oona pen-nah

... stamps
... dei francobolli
👄 day franko-bol-lee

... felt-tip pens
... dei pennarelli
👄 day pen-narel-lee

... colored pencils
delle matite colorate
👄 dellay mateetay coloratay

matite

. a key ring
. un portachiavi
👄 oon portah-ee-avee

... comics
... dei fumetti
👄 day foomayt-tee

97

... a box una scatolina
👄 oona skatoh–leenah

... a fridge magnet
una calamita da frigorifero
👄 oona kalameetah dah freego–reefayroh

... a CD un CD
👄 oon cheedee

How much is that?
Quanto costa?
👄 kwanto kostah

Italian kids, and adults, have always been mad about Disney comics. But did you know that most of the characters have Italian names you wouldn't recognise? Mickey Mouse is **Topolino** ("little mouse"), Goofy is **Pippo**, Donald Duck is **Paperino** ("little duck") and Huey, Dewey and Louie are **Qui, Quo, Qua**!

Money talks

How much pocket money do you get?
Quanta paghetta prendi?
👄 kwantah pagayttah prayndee

I only have this much
Io ho solo questi soldi
👄 eeo oh solo kwestee soldee

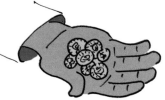

Can you lend me ten euros?
Mi presti dieci euros?
👄 mee praystee deeaychee yooro

No way!
Neanche per sogno!
👄 nayankay payr sonyeeo

Money talk

Italian money is the **euro** (pronounced *ayoo-roh*).
A euro is divided into 100 **centesimi** (*chayntayseemee*).

Coins: 1, 2, 5, 10, 20, 50 **centesimi**

1, 2 **euro**

Notes: 5, 10, 20, 50, 100 **euro**

Make sure you know how much you are spending before you blow all your pocket money at once!

GROWN UP TALK

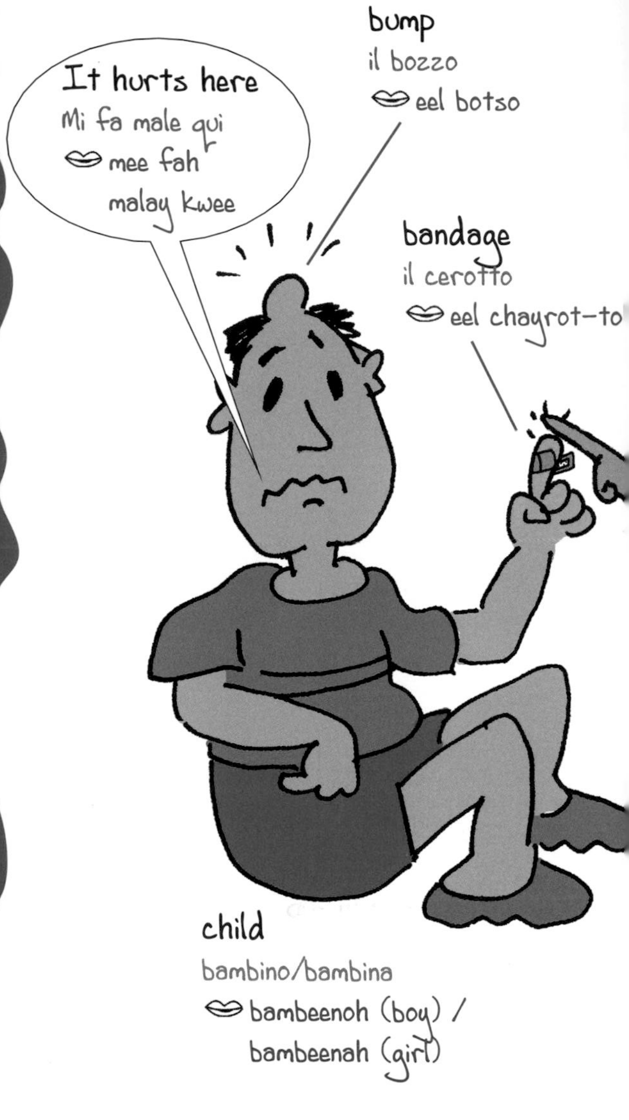

GROWN UP TALK

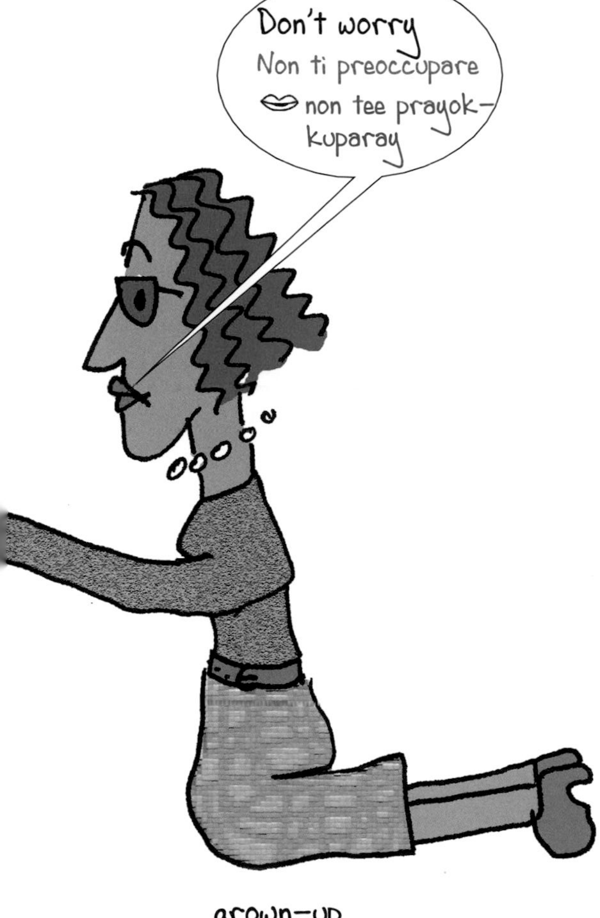

grown-up
adulto
adoolto

Help!

Something has broken
Si è rotto qualcosa
👄 see ay rot-to kwalkozah

Please
Per favore
👄 payr favoray

Can you help me?
Può aiutarmi?
👄 pwoh aeeootarmee

Where's the mailbox?
Dov'è la buca delle lettere?
👄 dovay lah booka dayl-lay lay-tayray

Where are the toilets?
Dov'è il bagno?
👄 dovay eel banyeeo

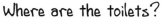

I can't manage it
Non ci riesco
👄 non chee ree-aysko

Could you pass me that?
Mi passi quello?
👄 mee pas-see kwayl-lo

What's the time?
Che ore sono?
👄 kay oray sonoh

Come and see
Vieni a vedere
👄 veeaynee ah vaydayray

May I look at your watch?
Mi fa vedere sul suo orologio
👄 mee fah vaydayray sool
soo-o orolojeeo

Lost for words

... my ticket
... il mio biglietto
👄 eel meeo
   bilyee-ayt-to

I've lost ...
Ho perso ...
👄 oh payrso

... my parents
... i miei genitori
👄 ee meeay
   jayneetoree

... my phone
... il mio
telefonino
👄 eel meeo
taylayfoneenoh

... my shoes
... le mie scarpe
👄 lay meeay skarpay

... my money ... i miei soldi
👄 ee meeay soldee

... my sweater
... la mia maglia
👄 lah meeah malyeeah

... my watch
... il mio orologio
👄 eel meeoh orolojeeo

... my jacket ... la mia giacca
👄 lah meeah jeeak-kah

how this page to adults who can't seem to make themselves clear (it happens). They will point to a phrase, you read what they mean, and you should all understand each other perfectly.

Non ti preoccupare
Don't worry

Siediti qui
Sit down here

Come ti chiami di nome e di cognome?
What's your name and surname?

Quanti anni hai?
How old are you?

Di dove sei?
Where are you from?

Dove sei alloggiato/a?
Where are you staying?

Cos'è che ti fa male?
Where does it hurt?

Sei allergico/a a qualcosa?
Are you allergic to anything?

È proibito
It's forbidden

Devi essere accompagnato/a da un adulto
You have to have an adult with you

Vado a cercare qualcuno che parli l'inglese
I'll get someone who speaks English

time
l'ora
lorah

EXTRA STUFF

Knock, knock.

Who's there?

Uno.

Uno who?

Unos where I got this crummy joke!

uno   👄 oonoh

due   👄 doo-ay

tre   👄 tray

quattro   👄 kwat-troh

cinque   👄 cheenkway

sei   👄 say

ette
🔊 sayt-tay

tto
🔊 ot-toh

ove
🔊 novay

ieci
🔊 deeaychee

ndici
🔊 oondeechee

odici
🔊 dodeechee

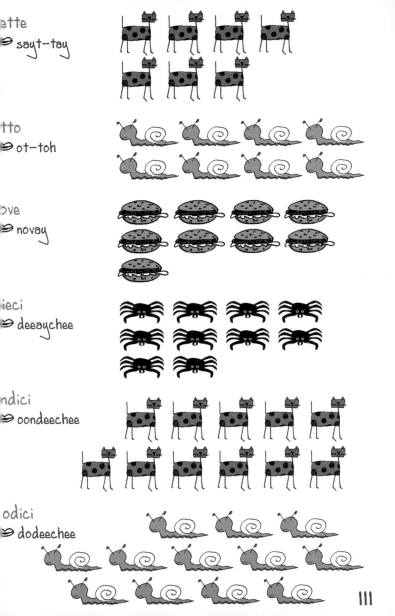

111

tredici 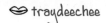 traydeechee

quattordici  kwat-tordeechee

quindici  kweendeechee

16	sedici	*saydeechee*
17	diciassette	*deechas-set-tay*
18	diciotto	*deechot-toh*
19	diciannove	*dechan-novay*
20	venti	*vayntee*

If you want to say "twenty-two," "sixty-five," and so on, you can just put the two numbers together like you do in English:

| 22 | **ventidue** | *vaynteedooay* |
| 65 | **sessantacinque** | *sayss-santacheenkway* |

This works except if you're saying "twenty-one," "sixty-one," and so on. Then you need to remove the final letter from the first number:

| 21 | **ventuno** (not **ventiuno**) | *vayntoonoh* |
| 61 | **sessantuno** (not **sessantauno**) | *sayss-santoonoh* |

30	trenta	*trayntah*
40	quaranta	*kwarantah*
50	cinquanta	*cheenkwantah*
60	sessanta	*sayssayntah*
70	settanta	*sayt-tantah*
80	ottanta	*ot-tantah*
90	novanta	*novantah*
100	cento	*chentoh*

113

Y ou might notice that Italians wave their hands a lot when they speak. What you won't realize is that not all flapping and waving means the same. Try looking out for some of these:

"What do you want?"

"Say that again"

"Are you crazy?"

"He's changed his mind

1,000 mille *meel-lay*

a million *un milione* *oon meel-lyonay*

a gazillion! *un fantastiliardo!* *oon fantasteeylardoh*

March	marzo	*martsoh*
April	aprile	*apreelay*
May	maggio	*madjoh*

June	giugno	*joonyoh*
July	luglio	*loolyoh*
August	agosto	*agostoh*

September	settembre	*set-tembray*
October	ottobre	*ot-tobray*
November	novembre	*novembray*

December	dicembre	*deechaymbray*
January	gennaio	*jen-nayoh*
February	febbraio	*feb-brayoh*

117

primavera *preemavayrah*

SPRING

estate *estatay*

SUMMER

autunno *owtoon-noh*

FALL

inverno *eenvernoh*

WINTER

118

Monday	lunedì	*loonaydee*
Tuesday	martedì	*martaydee*
Wednesday	mercoledì	*merkolaydee*
Thursday	giovedì	*jovaydee*
Friday	venerdì	*vaynayrdee*
Saturday	sabato	*sabatoh*
Sunday	domenica	*domayneekah*

By the way, school starts at around 8.30 a.m. for most children in Italy and ends around 1.00 p.m., but they also have to go to school on Saturday morning.

Good times

It's ...
Sono ...
👄 sonoh

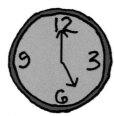

(five) o'clock
le (cinque)
👄 lay (cheenkway)

quarter after (two)
le (due) e un quarto
👄 lay (dooay) ay oon kwartoh

quarter to (four)
le (quattro) meno un quarto
👄 lay (kwat-troh) maynoh
    oon kwartoh

half past (three)
le (tre) e mezzo
👄 lay (tray) ay medzoh

120

five after (ten)

le (dieci) e cinque

👄 lay (deeaychee)
    ay cheenkway

twenty after (eleven)

le (undici) e venti

👄 lay (oondeechee)
    ay vayntee

ten to (four)

le (quattro) meno dieci

👄 lay (kwat–troh)
    maynoh deeaychee

twenty to (six)

le (sei) meno venti

👄 lay (say) maynoh vayntee

W atch out for "one o'clock." It's a bit different from the other times. If you want to say "It's one o'clock" you have to say **È l'una** *(ay loonah)*. "It's half past one" is **È l'una e mezza** *(ay loonah ay medzah)*, and so on.

morning
la mattina
👄 lah mat–teenah

midday
mezzogiorno
👄 medzojorrnoh

afternoon
il pomeriggio
👄 eel pomayreedjoh

evening la sera
👄 lah sayrah

midnight
mezzanotte
👄 medzanot–tay

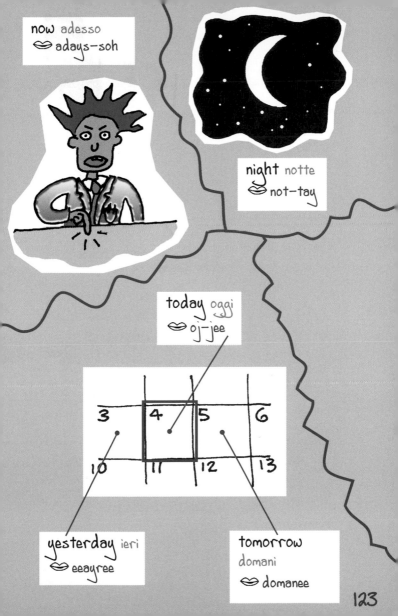

123

Weather wise

Can we go out?
Possiamo uscire?
👄 pos–seeamoh oosheerau

It's hot
Fa caldo 👄 fah kaldoh

It's cold
Fa freddo
👄 fah frayd–doh

It's a horrible day
Fa cattivo tempo
👄 fa kat–teevoh taympoh

It's raining basins!

When it rains heavily in Italy, people say it's "raining basins": **Piove a catinelle** (*peeovay ah kateenayl-lay*). A well-known saying is **Cielo a pecorelle acqua a catinelle**, or "Small sheep in the sky means basins of water." "Small sheep" are fluffy clouds!

It's windy
C'è vento
👄 chay vayntoh

It's sunny
C'è il sole
👄 chay eel solay

It's raining
Piove
👄 peeovay

It's snowing
Nevica 👄 nayveekah

I'm soaked
Sono fradicio
👄 sono fradeecheeo

It's nice Fa bel tempo
👄 fah bel taympoh

125

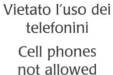

Signs of life

altezza minima

minimum height

Vietato l'uso dei telefonini

Cell phones not allowed

Vietato l'ingresso

No Entry

Vietato ai minori di 18 anni

Under 18s not allowed

126

Vietato ai
maggiori di 5 anni

Over 5s not allowed

FUORI
USO

OUT OF
ORDER

PRIVATO

PRIVATE